SIMPLICITY
IN LIFESTYLE

By
The Most Reverend John F. Whealon, D.D., S.S.L., ST.L.
Archbishop of Hartford

CATHOLIC AUTHORS PRESS
Hartford, Connecticut

First published in April, 1990
Copyright ©2009 Catholic Authors Press, Hartford CT
Simultaneously published in Canada
www.CatholicAuthors.org
ISBN: 978-0-9783198-8-5

CONTENTS

SIMPLICITY IN LIFESTYLE

INTRODUCTION

INTRODUCTION

Simplicity of living is now a challenge for every American follower of Christ.

Practical ideas about simplifying lifestyle are needed by every Christian in this affluent nation. I write about this subject with hesitation. A priest or bishop, and even more a woman or man under a religious vow of poverty, does not know personally the unending money problems faced by lay people in contemporary United States of America. We also feel the unending barrage of commercial advertisements telling people that happiness consists of buying more, having more, selling more, making more. But the person in religion is spared the financial worries and pressures of the laity.

There is much wisdom in the Gospels and the Church's tradition, available to help modern Catholics develop proper values in an affluent materialistic society. The impact of all this can be overwhelming, even devastating, on a person's value system, lifestyle, prayer life and spiritual growth. I suspect that many people would like to hear ideas about the Gospel teachings on simplicity in living. That is what I hope to do in this booklet.

SIMPLICITY IN LIFESTYLE

PART ONE

Background

PART ONE

This does seem to be a teachable moment for simplicity in living since materialism seems to have become total in modern society. Every day the typical American is exposed to approximately 3,000 commercial messages, from newspapers to billboards. The number of commercial messages transmitted by broadcast and print media doubled between 1967 and 1982, and may double again by 1997. The sense of clutter is especially intense on television. Because 30 seconds of prime time can cost an advertiser hundreds of thousands of dollars, there is a shift to 15-second formats. Ads of four, eight or more follow consecutively. Even the ads in the Sunday newspaper illustrate the commercial overload.

THE CHALLENGE FROM "ECONOMIC JUSTICE FOR ALL"

The Pastoral on Economics challenges us to examine our own priorities in money, possessions, and lifestyle. The text is a challenge for the ordinary reader. It is directed not only towards an understanding of its message, but also towards an examination of one's own priorities in living, use of money, and attachment to the things and possessions of this world. The document makes it clear that justice for the poor of our society and the rest of the world depends on the reordering of values and on the simple lifestyle of individual believers who live as the Gospel expects. For all of us – bishops and clergy, religious and lay people – that is a personal challenge.

SIMPLICITY IN LIFESTYLE

THE EXAMPLE OF OUR LORD JESUS

We who are committed to following the Christian way must give thought to the ideal of living as simply as possible. It is helpful to consider how the Master lived in this world. Jesus' way of life was simple to the point of austerity. The Son of the Almighty was born in a stable, laid in a manger, and wrapped with swaddling clothes. His life at Nazareth was certainly laborious and without luxuries. During his public life, Jesus stated: "The foxes have lairs, the birds in the sky have nests, but the Son of Man has nowhere to lay His Head" (Mt. 8:20). Stripped of garments, He died on a cross and was buried in another's grave.

Does this mean the follower of Christ must go to such lengths? No – we can never reach the perfection of that life. But it does mean that we must be "poor in spirit", simple in lifestyle, not attached to the things of this world. A wealthy person can have such poverty of spirit and can use wealth to accomplish great good for others. Conversely, a poor person without the virtue of poverty can be materialistic.

THE EXAMPLE OF FRANCIS OF ASSISI

The example of St. Francis of Assisi has much to say to younger as well as older Catholics. Francis was the talented son of a wealthy merchant who bought his child the finest clothing that money could buy. The young man went through a conversion, publicly gave the expensive clothes back to his father, and began a life of simple, poor, joyful following of Christ. With men and women Franciscan followers, he lived in harmony with God's creation and gave an example that is needed even more in our present society.

ADDED REASONS FOR SIMPLICITY IN LIFESTYLE

Concern and care for the poor must be important for Catholics and all Christians of this society. We have a problem because of the stark contrast between the lifestyle of the First World, including the United States, and the lifestyle of the people in the Third World. While a large number of Third World people suffer from malnutrition, many Americans eat and drink too much.

There are many reasons why all Christians, led and encouraged by clergy and religious, should adopt a simple lifestyle. Those reasons include a stewardship of the natural resources of this planet; an ecological concern not to pollute the air or water; a resolution not to harass nature with litter, garbage, or noise; and the demand of social justice, the "cry of the poor."

HOW MUCH OF THIS WORLD'S GOODS DO WE NEED?

The dominant motive for consciously cultivating a simple lifestyle is for Christians the powerful example and clear teaching of their Lord. The purpose of such a lifestyle is so that we may share more with those who have less. One obstacle to such simplicity is the common thinking that "my wealth is mine. I worked hard for it and have the right to do with it as I wish." The Gospel says "no" to this. We have the right to live in modest comfort and to plan reasonably for the future of ourselves and our dependents. However, the use of our surplus wealth must be measured with consideration of the basic needs of others which are not being met.

The Danger of Having Too Much

The words of the Letter to Timothy speak to us in Connecticut today: "We brought nothing into this world, nor have we the power to take anything out. If we have food and clothing, we have all that we need. Those who want to be rich are falling into a temptation and a trap. They are letting themselves be captured by foolish and harmful desires which drag people down to ruin and destruction. The love of money is the root of all evil." (1 Timothy 6:7-10) It is refreshing to know these ideas, about the proper way to judge and use the things of this world, so abundant in our society. But how can a person go about simplifying a lifestyle?

There are Americans, unhappy with slavery to things, disillusioned by an unsatisfactory excursion into the "paradise" of materialism. They have learned that more is not better, and that things really do not bring happiness. Haunted by the realization that we are being unjust to the world's poor and powerless, knowing that we are polluting planet earth to a dangerous degree, sensing that there is a great difference between the Gospel and the way we live. Following the teachings of Jesus Christ, some Americans perhaps are ready to take a bold step towards a lifestyle that is satisfying, ecologically acceptable and consistent with the demands of social justice.

SIMPLICITY
IN LIFESTYLE

PART TWO

Using the Good Things
in Moderation

PART TWO

Many of the ideas which I give you about developing a simple lifestyle are taken from a little book written by a brother bishop. Its title is *Living Like a King*. Written by Edward W. O'Rourke, Bishop of Peoria, it is published by the Templegate Publishers (302 East Adams St., Springfield, IL 62701). If you are serious about changing your approach to living, this book would be a practical help.

What are the essentials we need to live successfully and happily? The list is not a long one. Food, clothing, shelter, transportation, education, recreation and medical care are essential for the well-being of all people. If we have these, we have what we need to live.

Our problem in the U. S. A. is not so much having these essentials – as having them to excess. An extravagant use of these essentials in a hungry, needy world is obscene. The parable of Dives and Lazarus is being replayed and we are Dives, with only the crumbs from our tables going to the poor.

Our individual needs should be met in a manner that shows concern for the needs of others and for the environment. Our choices of what we have and what we buy should show a balanced appreciation of values. In lifestyle and possessions we should stress quality and not quantity. We should consider religious as well as practical considerations.

The size of our problem is shown by the size of

our people. While nearly half the human race suffers from malnutrition, obesity is a major health hazard in the United States of America. Here, over half the population weighs at least ten percent above ideal weight. Twenty-five percent of adult men and thirty-five percent of adult women in this nation are twenty percent above their ideal weight.

A reasonable lifestyle, then, must mean less consumption of food. It must also call for a reduction in the use of food additives and the degree of refinement of food. Sugar, white bleached flour, soft drinks and various sweetened and salted foods add calories, expense, and few useful nutrients to our diet. These are a partial cause of obesity, tooth decay, high blood pressure, and heart disease. They are also costly. Less refined, more nearly natural foods (such as fruits, vegetables, lean meat, fish, whole wheat and dairy products) are more economical approaches to a balanced diet.

Gardening is an excellent means of producing high quality vegetables and foods at minimal costs. Food budgets can also be stretched by buying directly from food producers, through farmers' markets and producers' cooperatives.

To be questioned is the need for mothers to buy costly baby foods rather than preparing the same by cooking and crushing fresh vegetables and fruits. Also to be questioned is the justice of Americans spending nearly three billion dollars a year on pet foods in a world where most of our fellow human beings lack sufficient food. A person who buys pet food for a dog or cat could well resolve to match that expense with donations to the famine victims in Ethiopia or elsewhere.

A further problem for us Americans is our prodigal use of clothing. Pressured by advertising and influenced by peers, many Americans buy clothing which they do not need and accept styles which are uncomfortable and costly. Though not many go so far as Imelda Marcos, many of us have closets overflowing with too many shoes, suits, dresses, sweaters, coats, hats, pocketbooks, etc. The cost of energy is causing changes in the size and construction of homes and in the use of heaters and air conditioners. More extensive use of insulation and more efficient approaches to heating and cooling are means of reducing energy costs. We should not expect to have a year-round temperature of 72 degrees in our home. The house should be cooler in the winter and warmer in the summer. The less we use heat and air-conditioning, the more we are living simply.

American extravagance is most conspicuous in our choice of transportation. Now most Americans after age 16 cannot picture life without the convenience of an automobile. Yet an automobile consumes two-and-one-fourth times as much energy per passenger as does a bus. Automobiles are the greatest single cause of air pollution in our nation. It is fairly obvious, then, that a more simple lifestyle should mean a lesser use of automobiles, more car pooling, greater use of public transportation, more bicycling and more walking. This is a challenge especially for the two-, three-, and four-car families of our society.

A simple lifestyle calls for lesser purchasing of recreation by watching others, and more do-it-yourself recreating. Creating your own music, sharing a sport or game with a spouse or friend, going for a walk in the park, reading a good book, are inexpensive, healthy and generally satisfying forms of recreation. Exercise is commendable. But most exercise gadgets are of little value and are soon abandoned. Many commercialized recreation, such as watching others at a sports activity, often exhaust and irritate the person, rather than adding to his or her joy and well-being. The word "recreation" means to re-create or rebuild the person. Passive recreation fails to re-create the person for the tasks ahead.

No rational person will deliberately neglect essential medical care. On the other hand, many of the nonprescription medications consumed by Americans are either harmful or ineffective. The fewer medications we take in life, the better for us.

Our food, clothing, shelter, transportation, recreation, and medical care should, if wisely used, advance our well-being and reduce our expenditures. The key to this is a combination of moderation and prudence. For most of us, a return to natural foods and fabrics, more carefully planned housing, more limited use of heating and cooling, a reduced use of automobiles, more creative recreation, and a minimal use of medications would noticeably improve our quality of living.

For anyone living in the U.S.A. of our times, life has become incredibly complicated. On television and radio we can be overwhelmed by thousands of attractive ideas every day. A visit to the local supermarket, department store or drug store means a survey of aisle after aisle of available products. Like the child in the candy store, we are surrounded by too much.

We must simplify. The challenge then becomes how much we simplify. The Gospel tells us to beware of having too much, of identifying our treasures in life with the things of this world. The Gospel says to lay up our treasures in heaven.

Somehow the challenge for the follower of Christ is to go through life with less, rather than more. Poverty of spirit is the first beatitude. But we, like our ancestors, worry about paying bills and having enough for our old age. We are pressured by the government to pay income tax. And yet, now as for 20 centuries, the Lord tells us to beware of money – to fear becoming too attached to things of this world.

There are good lessons to be learned from a New Englander who once lived at Walden Pond. Henry David Thoreau lived and meditated by Walden Pond on the genuine values in life. He wrote: "Simplicity, simplicity, simplicity! I say, let your affairs be as two or three, and not a hundred or a thousand; instead of a million count half a dozen, and keep your accounts on your thumb nail." And here we are, living in the computer age, the electronic age. How can we ever find the simplicity of Walden Pond, the simplicity of the Poor Man of Nazareth?

SIMPLICITY
IN LIFESTYLE

PART THREE

Why Simplify
Your Lifestyle?

PART THREE

I have already described the ecological reasons for a simplified lifestyle. It is true that we human beings, and especially we Americans, are living in a way that is despoiling planet earth and causing problems for future generations.

Special problems are being caused by those people who have surrendered to any of the four costly vices; tobacco, alcoholism, gambling and drug-addiction. The financial cost to people who indulge in these nonessential practices is huge, and the psychological and spiritual cost to self, family, and society is immeasurable. Experience has shown that preaching against these "vices" has little effect upon people caught in their grip. We must propose a different way of life, more attractive than these hazardous ones. We need to hold up a new lifestyle, one of simplicity, that shows respect for the body and, for God's creation. Why should we adopt a simple lifestyle? There are reasons beyond ecology. These reasons for simplicity come out of the Gospel itself. Anyone following a luxurious, materialistic, wasteful lifestyle can find no encouragement in the life and teachings of Christ Jesus. Jesus' way of life was simple almost to the point of austerity. St. Paul says that when God became man, God emptied self of the trappings of divinity. What kind of life did the Son of God accept? Paul described it as the life of a slave leading to the death of a slave (Philippians 2:5-11). Jesus was born in a stable, laid in a manger, wrapped in swaddling clothes. He was in infancy a refugee, living in a country of exile. His life at Nazareth was without luxuries, marked by hard work. Excavations have shown the poverty of Nazareth in New Testament times. During his public life Jesus stated, "The foxes have lairs, the birds of the sky have nests, but the Son of Man has nowhere to lay his head" (Matthew 8:20) "Jesus died a criminal's death on the cross, stripped of his garments, and was buried in someone else's grave. Born in another's cave, he was buried in another's grave.

On the other hand, Jesus enjoyed life. He did not hesitate to join in weddings and other celebrations. Jesus was not so severe as the Pharisees in interpreting the rules for sabbath rest and fasting. Jesus appreciated the beauty of nature, the joys of friendship, the glory of the temple in Jerusalem. The example of Jesus indicates that luxury is not the way to follow, but that beauty and simplicity are to be the pattern for living.

In fact, the gospel message is punctuated with harsh words for people attached to wealth, and with support for the poor in spirit. In Luke's Gospel we read, "But woe to you rich, for your consolation is now" (6:24). Even more blunt is the parable of the rich man and poor Lazarus. The rich man not only lived luxuriously, he was unconcerned about the sufferings of Lazarus. The rich man was punished with eternal condemnation (Luke 16:19-31). In the parable there is an obvious parallel to affluent individuals and nations who show no concern for the abject poverty of millions in the world, and Pope John

Paul II draws this parallel regularly.

Jesus showed at all times a special love for the poor, the heartbroken, and the ill. In his first sermon, as described by Luke, Jesus identified himself with the classic description of the Messiah: "The spirit of the Lord is upon me; therefore he has anointed me. He has sent me to bring glad tidings to the poor, to proclaim liberty to captives, recovery of sight to the blind, and release of prisoners" (Isaiah 61: 1-2, cf. Luke 4: 16-18) "In telling his followers whom to invite into their houses, Jesus said: "Whenever you give a lunch or dinner, do not invite your friends or brethren or relatives or wealthy neighbors. They might invite you in return and thus repay you. No, when you have a reception, invite the beggars and crippled, the lame and the blind. You should be pleased that they cannot repay you, for you will be repaid in the resurrection of the just" (Luke 14:12-13).

Jesus expects us to recognize him in the person of the poor. In describing the Last Judgment, Jesus says we will be judged positively if we have seen him in the poor and discriminated (Matthew 25:40).

Jesus made it clear that for his followers the real values lie above the things of this world. The Master said: "Stop worrying, then, over questions like 'What are we to eat, what are we to drink, what are we to wear?' The unbelievers are always running after these things. Your heavenly Father knows all that you need. Seek first his Kingship over you, his way of holiness, and all these things will be given you besides" (Matthew 6:31-33). Material possessions and physical pleasures are not evil. However, they may so dominate our thoughts that we neglect the more precious eternal values.

Why should we adopt a simplified lifestyle? A powerful reason for the Christian is simply the example and teachings of Jesus Christ. By word and example Jesus teaches us to use the things of this world with cautious moderation, and to be quick to share what we have with people in need.

The mission of Jesus was first to the poor and alienated. He lived among them, cared for their needs, loved them, and never looked down upon them. Our Lord expects us, his followers, to show the same love for the poor, the suffering, the alienated ones in our modern society. The Lord expects us to find and recognize his face in the poor.

All this calls for a life-style that is simple – a life-style that considers the needs of others, especially the poor, as much as our own needs. Because original sin is alive and well among us, such a way of living is very difficult. But that is the way of a follower of Christ.

I am setting down ideas about simplifying lifestyle, about enjoying life more while having less. Many Americans now connect happiness with having more possessions. Yet the Gospels and the experience of past generations teach that happiness is never bought, and is usually connected with having less than having more. Even in our expensive times the best things in life are free and the poor in spirit are the blessed, happy people.

Most Americans are concerned about getting enough money to pay their bills. Therefore the emphasis∑ is only on getting a raise, finding a better job, getting a better return on investments. Certainly it is a totally different approach to ask if the emphasis should be on having less and not more, on reducing money worries by simplifying as much as reasonably possible. That is the goal of this Pastoral – to see if a simple lifestyle, so different from the American acquisitive spirit, can lead to peace, holiness and happiness.

SIMPLICITY IN LIFESTYLE

PART FOUR

Why Do You Go Shopping?

PART FOUR

Recently the *Wall Street Journal* published a thorough analysis of motives of people for shopping. This section is a religious explanation of that analysis printed on July 30, 1987.

In the first half of this century, people went shopping only when they had to purchase a needed item. But since World War II a dramatic change in shopping habits has taken place in this country. Now many people really don't need what they are shopping for. Often they don't even know what they're after. Some buy things they never or rarely use; many buy and then return what they bought and then buy again and return that. Our ancestors would be amazed at our buying habits, and at the abundance available in any department or drug store.

There were many jokes about the shoe collection of Imelda Marcos. However, anyone of us whose closet is filled with superfluous clothing has no reason to laugh at the unfortunate Mrs. Marcos. Shoppers' behavior has been a major driving force for the economy. Shopping has become, arguably, the nation's favorite pastime next to watching television. Adults, both women and men, average about six hours a week doing their shopping. The time spent shopping is far more than the average hours a week spent gardening, reading books, golfing, and playing with children.

This increase in shopping has developed even though most women are now working, and people can conveniently order things through home shopping services. As inflation has continued, the shopping spree has gone on, pushing consumer debt to record highs and the savings rate to record lows. Economists, we are told, amazed at the shopping habits of Americans, wonder what has kept them going for so long, and periodically predict they will exhaust themselves and collapse under the weight of their possessions or debts. But even if shoppers do slow down, few economists expect that people will do something so dire as start saving money or stay home on Saturday or even Sunday afternoons.

Shopping has now taken on a life of its own. It has reached a pop-culture status with bumper stickers that say "I shop, therefore I am," and "Born to Shop." Shopping for many has become more than just providing for necessary things. It is fulfilling other needs and people don't like to think about that.

But the modern shopping craze raises profound psychological questions. To go into debt without knowing why and how the money is spent is mindless. While truly compulsive shoppers are a minority, the number of people having difficulty controlling an impulse to buy is much larger. It has been described as a national problem.

Who are the typical American shoppers? Recent studies say about 70 percent of all adults visit a regional mall every week, and a neighborhood shopping center twice a week. On an average, everybody shops for groceries at least twice a week. More men are shopping now, and comprise almost one-third of the mall crowd. Males are becoming fashion-conscious. Teenage boys spend two hours a week shopping, compared to four hours for teenage girls. Even the elderly, with memories of the Great Depression fading, are making shopping their sport. Shopping has become a favorite of vacationers.

Increasingly, purchases are linked less and less closely to need. Now it is replacement for the sake of change. People buy new sheets not because the old ones are worn out, but because they are attracted to a new design or color. This has long been true of clothing, but now is spreading to other areas. Six years ago, 75 percent of hardware purchases were to replace items that had worn out. Now less than half are replacements.

Much purchasing is being done on impulse. Studies say that about 53 percent of groceries and 47 percent of hardware sales are impulse buying. A poll of 34,300 mall shoppers, asking the primary reason for their visit, showed that only 25 percent came to buy a specific item.

Why do so many people spend so much time shopping? The reasons are many and complex. According to shoppers and those who study them, shopping can mean different things to different people. It can ease loneliness and boredom. It can be a sport, filled with the thrill of a hunt. It can provide escape, fulfill fantasies, relieve depression. Here are some of the reasons given.

Alleviating loneliness. For some people, shopping seems to be a substitute for a relationship. The most avid shoppers are the single, the widowed, and the divorced in our society. When such a person has nothing else to do, there is always the mall and the people there.

Dispelling boredom. Shopping is tailor-made for a generation that thrives on bright colors and visual distractions. At the mall there is always something new. If a person gets tired of clothes after a few months, there is an urge to get something new. Something new brings a short-lived thrill. It is something to talk about.

Shopping as a sport. Some people find a challenge in getting something at the cheapest price. So they will go to several stores in search of the best bargain. They cull through endless racks of items to find the largest discount. With the intensity of a fanatic they follow the sales. The stores clearly invite such people by advertising sale after sale, and discount a discounted item to the point where there is no longer any true price. Newspapers and magazines have become more shopping guides than papers of news and information.

Shopping as an escape. Some working people admit that for them shopping is a pleasant, mind-numbing behavior. It is a little vacation from daily tasks. Some women say they can go into a home-decorating store and find it a therapy.

Fantasy fulfillment. Stores in the malls are filled with the fantastic. There are stores presenting themselves as Banana Republic, filled with exotic items and pictures from anywhere but here. This appeals to the adventuresome spirit in people.

Relieving depression. Some people find that shopping, or even thinking of shopping, makes them feel better. The colors, the clothes, the music, the crowds – all these take their minds off their problems.

It is interesting to note that the credit card encourages people to spend more. In one recent study people were asked how much they would be willing to spend for a toaster. When a credit card was pictured nearby (as it is on many cash registers), they were willing to spend three times as much as when the credit cards were not advertised. Pictures of credit cards developed an almost Pavlovian response in those people.

A more recent article said the average American is subject to 5,000 commercials a day. To keep a spiritual balance in the midst of all this commercialism is a challenge. Consumers are caught in a trap of hedonism – an ever-spiraling and hopeless search for happiness through the acquisition of things. When the buyer inevitably finds that the last purchase has not met expectations, he or she says, "I'll just buy this one more thing." Then the cycle continues. All this commercialism is good for the economy, giving people jobs. But it is not good for people's minds or souls.

The follower of Jesus Christ knows that the Master warned against the dangers of money, against becoming attached to the things of this world. We are to lay up our treasures in heaven, not here on earth. We cannot serve both God and mammon.

Certainly the follower of Christ who for any reason joined the national shopping spree has wandered off the straight and narrow path. Our challenge in life is not how much we have, but how little baggage we carryon this journey. Our goal is not to become rich but to become poor, at least in spirit. Our ideal is simplicity in lifestyle.

With some hesitation I am writing on simplicity in living. The bishop, priest, or religious under a vow of poverty has comparatively few challenges in this area. We are expected to live simply. Our vow of celibacy, our low salary, our traditions make it easier to live by the Gospel ideal. We can have worries – but these are more about a parent than about oneself.

The lay person living in the world is in quite a different situation. For such a person, the high cost of living can be a constant worry, an unending pressure. Raising children is so expensive that some ungenerous married couples refuse the burden and deny the obligation. Further, the value structures of our American society proclaim that the real goals for living are making more money, having more possessions, finding more enjoyment. Who now believes in, or even talks about, fidelity or honesty or chastity? That is what the laity face every day.

So, for me to even write about simplicity in living may seem presumptuous. Yet the Gospel was not for bishops, priests and religious alone. I believe the Gospel has much to say to the single man or woman, to the married couple, caught up in the unending competitive struggle of modern living.

Though we think that now prices are high and inflation is crushing, probably our ancestors in life and in the faith had worries equally as pressing. Perhaps we really are much better off than they – but we don't know it. The challenge of the poor Jesus Christ is our challenge, as it was for them in their time. We are all tenants of time, pilgrims on this earth.

SIMPLICITY IN LIFESTYLE

PART FIVE

Four Poor People

PART FIVE

Here are the stories of four different people who decided to adopt a simple lifestyle in imitation of Jesus Christ. What they decided and how they lived can encourage us.

FRANCIS OF ASSISI

He was born and baptized in Assisi, Italy, about 1182. A bright, personable youth, he was nicknamed Francis ("the Frenchman") because his father was on a business trip to France when Giovanni Bernardone was born. The father was a prosperous cloth merchant. As a young man, Francis enjoyed the luxury and pleasures which wealth made possible. Somewhat a free spirit, he did not take studies or work seriously.

But at age 20 Francis experienced imprisonment and illness. He became mature, went through a conversion, and started giving away possessions to the poor. His father dispossessed him, and Francis publicly gave back to his father all the money and clothes he had received. Francis gave up family and possessions, and was joined by a few followers who caught his spirit of simple, joyful, grateful living. Thus began the process which led to the formation of the Franciscan Orders.

At Mass one day in 1208, the Gospel reading was taken from Matthew, Chapter 10: "As you go, make this announcement: 'The Kingdom of God is at hand'... The gift you have received, give as a gift. Provide yourselves with neither gold nor silver nor copper in your belts; no traveling bag, no change of shirt, no sandals, no walking staff." Francis took these words as the basic rule of his order. He and his brothers embraced poverty because they saw it as the root of the Gospel message, as the counsel on which the other evangelical counsels depend.

Francis said he was married to Lady Poverty. Called the most Christlike person since Christ, he founded also a Third Order for lay people living in the world, enabling them to follow the Franciscan way. Kings and queens have been Third Order members, or Secular Franciscans. And the Secular Franciscans continue in our times. Any true follower of Christ is at least a closet Franciscan.

The name of Francis of Assisi is almost synonymous with a simple, joyful, holy way of life. He was the "Little Poor Man of Assisi." The more he embraced poverty, the greater the freedom and joy he knew.

DOROTHY DAY

Much closer to our own times is Dorothy Day, convert to the faith, co-founder of *The Catholic Worker*, who died in 1980. As a seminarian during the 1940s I subscribed to the newspaper, worked on a *Catholic Worker* farm, and visited the first House of Hospitality on Mott Street in New York City.

Dorothy Day grew up as a rebellious intellectual, had an irregular marital history, as a single mother raised a daughter, and became an active Communist. Social justice was for her a burning concern. But the Hound of Heaven, the grace of God, led her to Christ and the Church. She dedicated her life to serving Christ in the poor, and with a homespun street person, a French peasant named Peter Maurin, founded the *Catholic Worker* Movement with its Houses of Hospitality. This was what we recognize as a soup kitchen and shelter. She worked at this during the Great Depression. *The Catholic Worker* Movement spread across the country and continues today also within the Archdiocese of Hartford.

The spirit of Dorothy Day is that of Matthew 25: to see the person of Christ in the poor of today and to serve the poor. There is no question but that Dorothy Day accepted poverty as a way of life just as wholeheartedly as did Francis of Assisi. She wrote these balanced words about simplicity in living: "I feel that all families should have the conveniences and comforts which modern living brings, and which do simplify life and give time to read, to study, to think and pray. And to work in the apostolate too. But poverty is my vocation, to live as simply and poorly as I can, and never cease talking and writing of poverty and destitution." She wanted to share the poverty and suffering of the poor. Her life and her writings remain an inspiration.

BISHOP BERNARD TOPEL

Here is the story of a bishop, recently

deceased, who decided to take the Gospel literally. As Bishop of Spokane he took part in the Second Vatican Council. Later he wrote: "During the Council, bishops often spoke of the Church as the Church of the poor. This troubled me because I do not see that we are. What has been wrong, I am convinced, is that those of us who should be giving leadership in following Christ's teaching have not been living the message of Christ the way we should be living it. We water it down. The salt has lost its savor."

Bishop Topel proceeded to sell his episcopal mansion and give the money to the poor. He did the same with his episcopal jewelry. He moved into a small four-room house in a low-income neighborhood of Spokane. Taking no salary, he lived on social security, grew his own vegetables, and purchased almost no clothing for himself.

When asked why he lived that way, Bishop Topel answered that it was a result of his prayer life. By word and example, Bishop Topel urged the affluent of his diocese to examine their lifestyle and to be more conscious of the missions and the poor. At the same time he told the poor to be grateful to God for their poverty, and to offer up their poverty to God as an expression of love.

MOTHER TERESA OF CALCUTTA

She is the most famous religious woman in the world, winner of the Nobel Prize. Remarkably, she is famous for her poverty and dedication to the poor. Mother Teresa was born in 1910, of Albanian parents, in Yugoslavia. Wanting to serve in India, she joined the Loreto nuns in Ireland because they were working in the Calcutta Archdiocese. In 1948 she asked to work in the Calcutta slums. She became an Indian citizen, and in 1950 started the Congregation of the Missionaries of Charity. The institution and works of this Congregation have expanded dramatically and are worldwide.

These sisters serve the most impoverished, the most abandoned of the poor in Calcutta and other cities of the world. The sisters deliberately choose a life of rigorous poverty, directing almost all their resources to the needs of the poor rather than to themselves. Mother Teresa further explains their motives: "We would not be able to understand and effectively help those who lack all, if we do not live like them." Also, "We must free ourselves to be filled with God. Even God cannot fill what is full."

Three of these examples are of people under public vows. There are in our society many good lay people who by choice are following a simple, poor lifestyle. But the laity do not receive attention or press on this question.

Certainly we in religion should be setting an example, as Bishop Topel says. Vowed celibacy without a simple lifestyle is no witness of living for the next world. When vowed celibacy is used to amass worldly possessions and live in high style, the person is living for this world, not the next, and has a major spiritual problem. Even for a religious the challenge to live in poverty is not easily met. We must keep trying, stay detached from possessions, and ask God's mercy for our failures.

We are all following Christ, the Poor Man of Nazareth, who emptied himself of the trappings of divinity and took on the way of life of a slave. Imitating that example, we must consider a personal lifestyle that keeps us free from attachment to the things of this world and that helps us serve Christ in the poor.

I have been offering ideas about the challenge of following the Poor Man of Nazareth while living in the most affluent state within the affluent United States of America. Daily we are overwhelmed with an abundance of goods and food. We are encouraged by thousands of advertisements every day to buy more, to have more, to get the latest and the best. We are told that the way to be really important is to own what everyone else has, and then more.

There are many people in Connecticut who are struggling to pay their bills, to keep their heads above water. They may benefit from these ideas, in case they are struggling to have luxuries and not necessities. There are other people in our state who have all the necessities they really need. These people can benefit much from these teachings if they are being challenged to look at their possessions in the light of the Gospel.

What do you need to live adequately? Really,

the essentials are not many:

- ✢ A roof over your head.
- ✢ Heat in the winter and coolness in the summer.
- ✢ Food and clothing for the body.
- ✢ Health care.
- ✢ A chance to develop in education and culture.
- ✢ Religious freedom.
- ✢ Some time for leisure and recreation.

It is not a long list, and much of it is not expensive, even in these days.

It is a milestone of wisdom in life when a person says: "I really have everything necessary for living. I thank God for that, I do not depend on any new thing to make me happy."

A problem is that, now in the U. S .A., people are concerned about the cost of living in a nursing home. So the tendency is to save for the unknown expensive future. And yet now the cost of nursing home care is so great that a person's life savings are exhausted in a few years. We are fortunate to have government support for such people made poor by the system. This is a humbling but literal way of following the poverty of Jesus Christ.

It is wisdom to say to yourself: "I have all I really need." It is greater wisdom to start asking yourself: "Do I have too much?" That question makes you think about the Gospel ideal of simplicity of living.

SIMPLICITY IN LIFESTYLE

SIMPLICITY IN LIFESTYLE

PART SIX

A Plan of Action

PART SIX

Those individuals and families wishing to simplify lifestyles may find the following plan of action helpful. Most people find it difficult to move in a single step from an affluent to a simple lifestyle. Many personal habits and peer pressures discourage such an abrupt change. So a gradual approach, following these steps, may be more realistic.

Step One: Get rid of unnecessary and superfluous items in your house. If your house or room is cluttered with things you have not used for years, do not need, and will not need, get rid of them. If your closet is overflowing, clean it out and give usable items to the poor. For a person trying to follow the simplicity of the Gospel, superfluous possessions become a problem. Judge yourself by how little you have rather than by how much you have.

Step Two: This is like the Tenth Station of the Cross: a deliberate stripping away of some things. To do this, aim at a five percent reduction in your consumption of goods and services. This can be accomplished rather painlessly and swiftly. A possible way to reach this goal is to attack any areas of addiction. Heavy cigarette smokers might at least reduce to one pack a day. This will greatly reduce health hazards and, of course, the cost of tobacco. Heavy drinkers of alcohol should at least resolve to limit the amount daily, or to take only wine or beer and these only with food. Beverages with lower alcoholic content are less costly than hard liquors. When taken with food the good effects begin to offset the bad effects of such consumption.

It goes almost without saying that any use of unnecessary drugs is incompatible with a simple lifestyle, even at this early stage. The goal should be to take as few over-the-counter drugs as possible. People afflicted with habits of drug dependency should look for professional help. The same is true for people addicted to gambling. If you gamble for fun, resolve to gamble only with friends. In this way the companionship will help to dignify and humanize the experience. The beneficiaries of your losses will be friends, not the Mafia. Further, gambling in the State Lottery should be incompatible with this stage of simplified living.

The automobile you drive should have a good miles per-gallon ratio. A scrutiny of your auto travel will indicate how many trips are unnecessary.

Study your clothing budget. Try for better quality clothing at modest costs, paying less attention to ephemeral fashions. Attempt to reduce the consumption of energy in your home. This will mean lower temperatures during the winter and a more saving use of appliances, including summertime air conditioners. Try, on a regular basis, to spend some family recreational time together, at home. This will reduce spending on recreation, and will help to strengthen the bonds among family members.

Most people who take this step are surprised to

find how easy it is. The results, in almost every case, are an increase in personal well-being and health, a greater appreciation of material things, and a more human outlook on other persons.

Step Three: This is the more severe test – a spiritual lifestyle. Begin to tithe – to give ten percent of your income back to God, with five percent to your parish and five percent to charities. It will be difficult to do this unless you are strongly motivated by religious reasons. A special closeness to Jesus Christ and an experience of freedom are among the rewards of this step.

Look to your food consumption. Do more home cooking: use fewer prepared foods. You may have the skill to make or repair clothing. Prefer laundering to dry cleaning.

In this step the person will try to walk or car pool, to restrict severely unnecessary journeys, to live in a smaller house or apartment, to prefer living in the inner city with public transportation rather than the suburbs.

Step Four: This is adopting a life of poverty.

This means carrying out, as best you can, the words of Jesus to "go, sell what you have, give it to the poor, and come, follow me." In this stage you should have a prudent spiritual director. Everyone needs leisure and the experience of culture and beauty in living. Some people at this stage opt for communal living with others of similar ideals, and become deeply involved in services to the poor. There are many beneficiaries of a person's simple living and giving.

These ideas about simplicity in living are related to the Catholic vision of reverence for all God's creation, especially human life in all its forms. In a way that I cannot express clearly, this ideal means a realization of the sacredness of all life and creation.

Part of that reverence for life is the Catholic teaching on human sexuality. The Church does not disapprove of sexuality, but sees it as a gift of God to be used in its fullness and completeness, as given by God. The Church says yes to sex in a way the modern society does not comprehend. Those who disapprove of sexuality are those who make it recreational, who surround it with chemicals and plastics in order to make it frustrated of its natural purpose. Our modern society is squeamish about sex and says no to its fullness.

We need to proclaim the full truth about the human person and the gift of human sexuality. We need to tell moderns that there is such a thing as safe sex. It is when a virginal man and woman marry and are faithful for life. There is a way of living marriage by God's plan, a way that will help to sanctify – and this is Natural Family Planning. We who live in this materialistic, sensual society have special challenges in following the Gospel. We can easily get discouraged by our imperfections and weaknesses. Our best prayer for this is the ancient "Kyrie eleison:" Lord, have mercy.

PART SIX

It helps also to keep before us the example of Jesus and of others who have deliberately simplified their lifestyle. I close with beautiful helpful words from the New Testament:

"Therefore, since we for our part are surrounded by this cloud of witnesses, let us lay aside every encumbrance of sin which clings to us and persevere in running the race which lies ahead; let us keep our eyes fixed on Jesus, who inspires and perfects our faith."

(Hebrews 12:1-2)

www.ingramcontent.com/pod-product-compliance
Lightning Source LLC
Chambersburg PA
CBHW021223020426
42331CB00003B/448